To Stephen for being brilliant

First published in the UK in July 2016 as "The Agile Team Onion"

Version 3

© Emily Webber 2023

ISBN 978-1-7393643-0-4

Published by: Tacit London Ltd

Designed by: Stephen Walker

Edited by: Giles Turnbull

All rights reserved. No part of this publication may be reproduced, sorted in a retrieval system, or transmitted in any form or by any means, electronic, mechanical, photocopying, scanning, recording or otherwise, without the copyright owner's prior permission.

Share this book

If you enjoyed this book, visit the website at teamonion.works, let other people know by sharing it with your social networks and message me on Twitter: @ewebber

The Team Onion

A model to keep teams small,
break down silos and create shared
responsibility across team boundaries.

By Emily Webber

Contents

1. **Introduction** — 5
   Who the Team Onion is for — 7
2. **The Team Onion solves lots of different problems** — 9
   The founding concepts behind the Team Onion — 10
3. **Overview of the Team Onion Model** — 21
   The model — 22
   The people in the layers — 23
   Team size and the onion layers — 24
4. **Creating your Team Onion** — 27
   The five steps to creating your Team Onion — 29
   Overlapping Onions — 38
   Workshop materials — 39
5. **Some example scenarios** — 41
   Building a new team from scratch: getting the right people involved — 42
   Team kick-off: coalescing a new team — 44
   Team Retrospective: breaking down silos and reducing communication overhead — 46
   Starting a new engagement: building a picture of who's who — 48
   Useful links — 50
   Complementary tools and approaches — 51
6. **References and thanks** — 53
7. **About the author** — 57

Introduction

A while back, I worked with an organisation a few years into its digital transformation. They had a few small multidisciplinary teams working on an essential service. Within the context of a wider organisation, those teams relied on multiple functional groups and processes to do their work. Each team had a mix of capabilities, regular insights from users, a backlog that responded to change, and a delivery rhythm. But they weren't able to get anything done.

They were pretty self-sufficient, but they needed approval from above and alignment from their peers before they could put anything live.

When I joined, I made it my mission to help one team get their service live. When I asked them how they worked with the functional groups above them in the hierarchy, they said those groups were blocking them. For example: the security team wouldn't let them put anything live on the internet, and the policy team wouldn't turn up to their all-day workshops.

When I spoke to the functional groups, the people the team accused of being blockers, they said they didn't understand what the team was doing, what was needed from them, and anyway, they were busy with other things. Why would they give up a day to participate? The lack of progress was no-one's fault; everyone said it was someone else's fault.

What was really going on was that everyone had different priorities and different ways of working; they didn't understand what was motivating other people in the organisation to behave in certain ways, causing friction. They didn't even understand what each other did. They hadn't been able to build empathy and a shared goal — typical siloed organisational behaviour.

The Team Onion was born as a way of bridging those silos, building empathy and helping the different teams and groups pull together in the same direction.

This book looks at problems the Team Onion can solve, helps you understand how to use it, and provides practical workshop templates and insightful stories from people who have used it successfully.

Who the Team Onion is for

The Team Onion model started life as something for Agile teams, but there's evidence that it works for all types of teams. It's flexible enough to use in lots of different scenarios.

Including:

People
who feel disconnected from other parts of the organisation

Teams
who feel overwhelmed by cognitive overhead

Team leads
setting up a new team or kicking off a new project

Consultants
starting a new engagement

Leaders
starting a new area of work

2

The Team Onion solves lots of different problems

The Team Onion is a lightweight yet powerful visualisation tool. It helps to keep teams small while delivering in the context of a larger organisation.

It is similar to a stakeholder map, but emphasises collaboration and framing people outside the core as an extension of the team. More on that later.

It helps to break down silos, foster good communication and collaboration, surface assumptions, build empathy and create shared ownership and responsibility for success. Using the model in a workshop format facilitates meaningful conversations about the capabilities, time commitment, collaboration and communication patterns needed for teams to be successful.

Teams that use the model will find that delivering value gets more manageable as they identify their extended team. People outside of the core team will have the opportunity to get involved and add real value when it's most needed.

The founding concepts behind the Team Onion

Concept 1: Silos stop work flowing.
If what a team creates can't get into the hands of the people who need to use it, they cannot create value.

Concept 2: Small teams can move faster.
They can communicate and collaborate more effectively. Conversely, big teams have a more significant communication overhead, slower decision-making, and a greater cognitive load.

The Team Onion makes the need for collaboration outside the core team explicit, to keep teams small and bridge silos.

Let's look at each of those founding concepts in a bit more detail.

Concept 1: Silos stop work flowing

Silos are the antithesis of empathy.

They make it hard for ideas and work to flow, for people to share valuable information and for decisions to be made quickly, which is far from ideal when an organisation is trying to get everyone to pull in the same direction. Conversely, when you bring people together with diverse experiences and viewpoints, your team will have fewer blind spots and benefit from a wider pool of knowledge.

You know you have silos when you hear people talking about a team as a blocker, rather than as people they are working with. These silos can lead to teams working against each other rather than collaboratively towards a common goal.

> # ‹Insert group name› are rubbish at…

Siloed language is when we blame faceless groups rather than work together.

Silos often exist in an organisation when teams are broken down into functions and work cannot be completed until it has been through many, or all, of these functions. Any time a piece of work has to be handed off to another team, it takes longer to complete. Not only does the team have to switch to the new work, but they also lose a lot of knowledge about the work.

In the book Implementing Lead Software Development: From Concept to Cash, Mary and Tom Poppendiek conservatively estimate that 50% of tacit knowledge is lost when work is handed over to another person or team not previously involved. In just a few handovers that can mean that much of the original intent and understanding has been lost.

0   1   2   3   4

● Tacit knowledge lost in handoffs

Breaking down silos with multidisciplinary teams

One way of reducing handovers and benefitting from increased diversity is to bring together those different functions into one team. A multidisciplinary (or cross-functional) team has all the knowledge, skills and experience that it needs to scope, design, create and support an initiative, product or service—working together to achieve an outcome, releasing value early and often.

The origin of the multidisciplinary team

Multidisciplinary teams are not a new idea – they have been used in healthcare since the 1970s.

Patients who have complex needs are treated by a team of people from different disciplines, working together to provide the most appropriate care. Multidisciplinary healthcare teams can create a more rounded approach to a problem and are less likely to be biased toward a one-sided solution.

If you've ever been in a hospital and seen a huddle of clinicians talking together in a corner, that's multidisciplinary healthcare in action.

"Cohesive teamwork improved communication between different levels of healthcare workers, and limited adverse events, improved outcomes, decreased the length of stay ... and yielded greater patient "staff" satisfaction." [1]

Or in simpler terms: multidisciplinary health teams get better results, send patients home from the hospital sooner, and everyone feels better about it.

Lots of organisations outside healthcare have adopted this model, moving away from functional silos where work is done in a vacuum or passed between departments; and towards the multidisciplinary team, where teams have all the capabilities they need to design, deliver, and deploy work without depending on other people and teams.

In the Agile Manifesto[2], which sets out the principles of Agile working, one principle speaks about bringing together the people making the work and the people making decisions:

"Business people and developers must work together daily throughout the project".

This principle is intended to reduce the handoffs, build understanding, reduce blind spots and speed up decision-making.

Bring in people you rely on early, build empathy and work together.

In around 2008 (in the days before Instagram), I worked on a project to launch a campaign website. The client was a large international company and the project was centred around giving away free samples of one of its products to people on nights out.

The campaign involved photographers taking photos of people and uploading them to the campaign website the next day, inviting people to share them on Facebook. Having multiple photographers upload images to the website made the client really nervous; it wasn't something they had done before, and they assumed that the security and compliance team would take too long to sign it off. They were worried, because there was limited time to get everything built, tested and live. They talked about how the security and compliance team "never signed anything off quickly".

As the project lead, the first thing I did was connect with the security and compliance team to find out who would be on the hook for signing off the website. Once we knew, I introduced them to the work and set up regular times to take them through what we were doing, decisions made along the way and get feedback to make sure that we met their needs.

By the time it came to getting sign off, it was very straightforward and almost instantaneous— the client was shocked, this was something they had never seen before.

Here's the thing: it's a lot to expect someone who has never seen your work before to put their name and reputation to it. Not only have they not had the chance to influence decisions, but they also have a long way to go to get their head around what you have built. If we had broken the compliance rules, the photos would not have gone live, and we would have to start again.

Connecting early and often to build a collaboration pattern shows empathy and helps everyone reach their goals faster.

Concept 2: Small teams can move faster

Teams aren't just made of people; they're made of relationships. The dynamics of those relations are really important. That includes how they interact with each other, their cultural norms, active conversations and shared history.

To function effectively in a team, each member needs to understand the relationships between themselves and the other people in the team, as well as those between everyone else in the team.

These relationships grow exponentially with new people; having 25 people on a team creates 300 relationships.

"As a team gets bigger, the number of links that need to be managed among members goes up at an accelerating, almost exponential rate. It's managing the links between members that gets teams into trouble."

— J. Richard Hackman, the Edgar Pierce Professor of Social and Organisational Psychology at Harvard University[3]

Adding more people to a team makes communication a more significant overhead. Decision-making slows down and cognitive load goes up. And adding one person doesn't just add one extra relationship; it adds many.

Aim for smaller teams

There is no ideal team size for every situation. No two scenarios are exactly the same, but a good rule of thumb often cited[4] with digital teams is seven, plus or minus two. That's a range of five to nine people. That keeps your relationships between 10 and 36.

5 people / 10 relationships

7 people / 21 relationships

9 people / 36 relationships

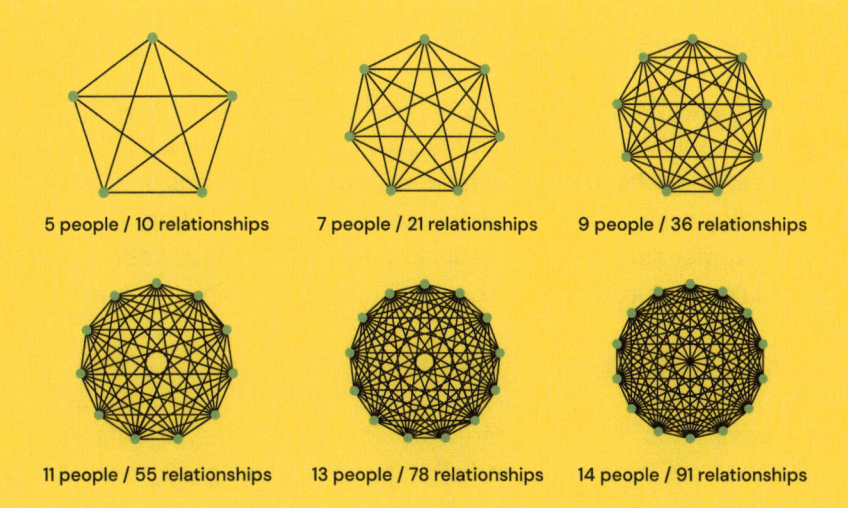

11 people / 55 relationships

13 people / 78 relationships

14 people / 91 relationships

Adding one person doesn't just add one extra relationship; it adds many.

Small teams with BIG work

Having all the capabilities you need in a team is easier when an organisation is small and people play mixed roles, but what about large organisations with whole functions dedicated to activities such as legal, policy, marketing, customer support and security? All the capabilities needed could mean teams of 50 people or more. Certainly not small.

Teams don't work in a vacuum

Teams need to be integrated into the broader organisation to deliver the most value and align its overarching goals. In small organisations where teams have easy access to most people they need to talk to, they manage this through quick conversations and alignment sessions. But where outcomes are more complex and the organisation more distributed, they need to work harder to make collaboration happen.

I've seen many organisations respond to this by shielding teams from the rest of the organisation. Or creating boards and "authorities" to sign off work from afar and assure that it fits with organisational standards and policies. This can create silos, slow down delivery and worse, lead to a blame culture.

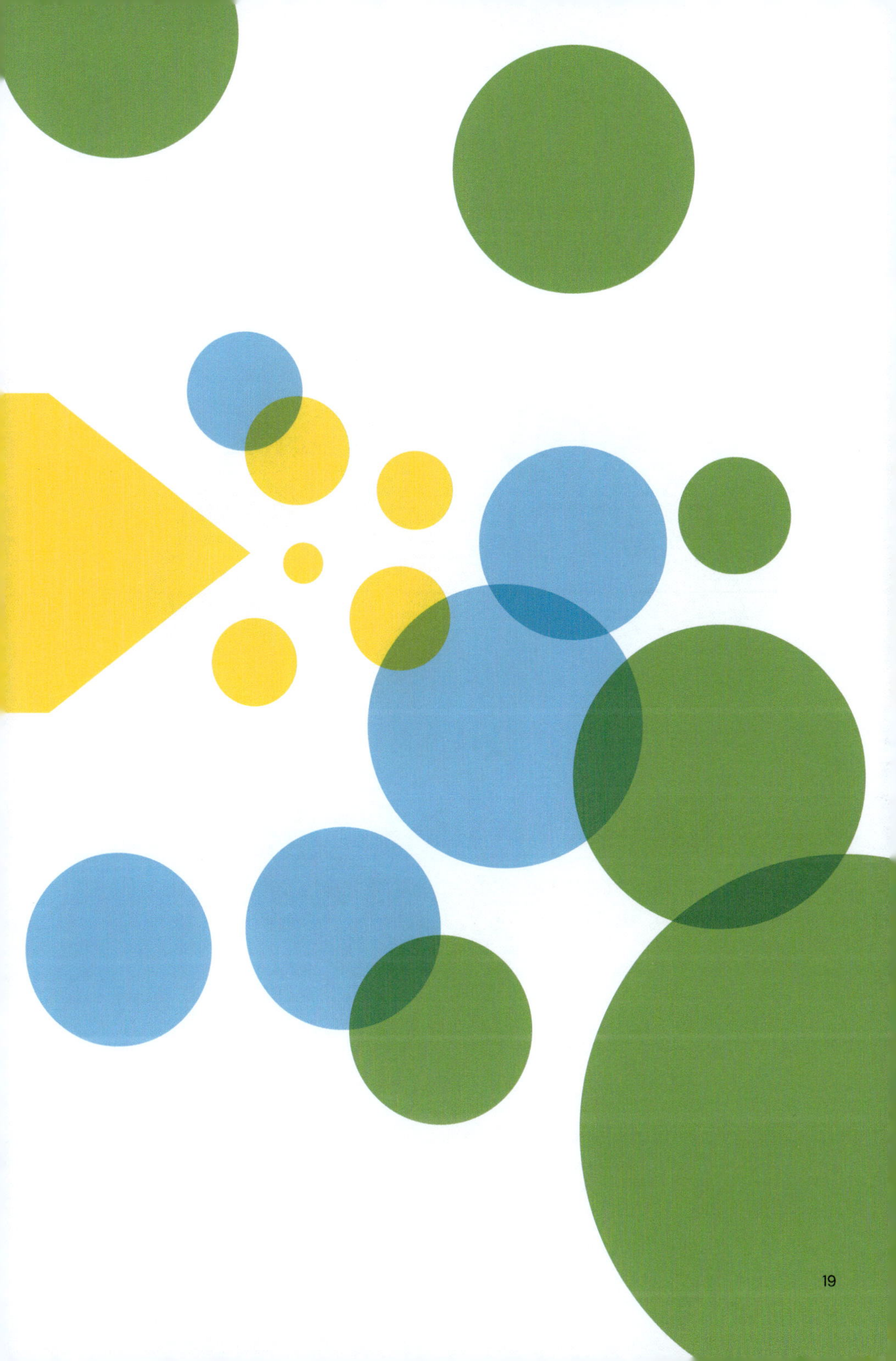

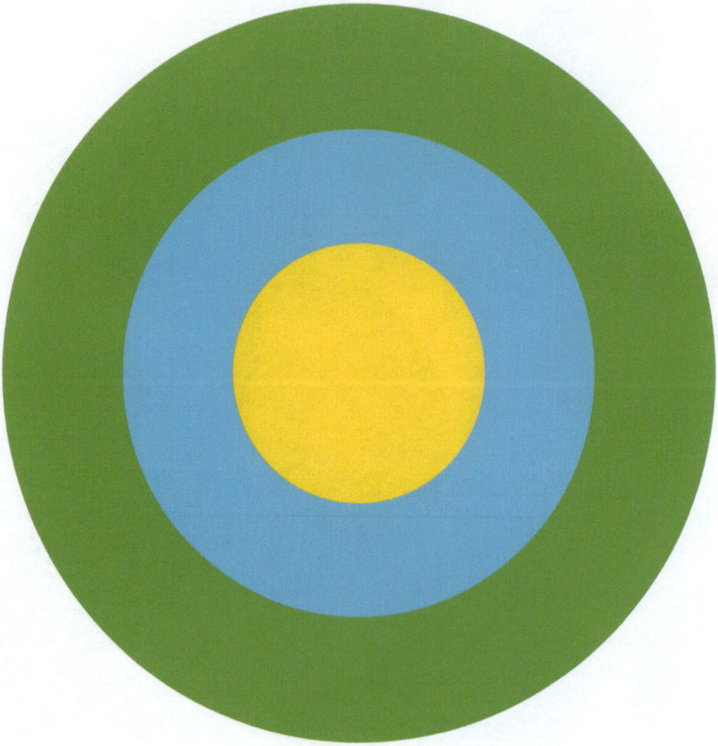

3

Overview of the Team Onion model

The Team Onion is a model and collaborative tool with co-created and co-owned outputs.

Its power is in the conversations around it, designed to uncover assumptions, make decisions, and identify actions requiring real-time, synchronous discussions.

The model should be co-created with a set of people who can make decisions and act on the outcomes. It should be considered a living artefact, changing over time.

The model

The Team Onion model is in three layers: the **core** team, regular **collaborators** and people who act as **supporters**.

Mapping out these layers helps everyone understand the team and the people it should regularly collaborate and communicate with.

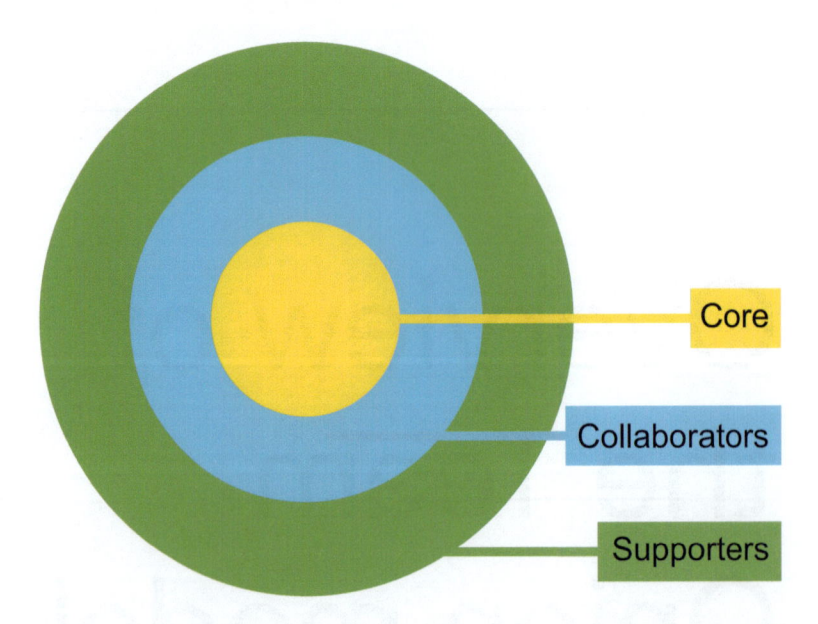

The people in the layers

When creating the layers, it's essential to have discussions about the capabilities, commitment, collaboration and communication for each person, in each layer;

- the **capabilities** they need to be successful, rather than roles
- time **commitment** from each team member
- **collaboration** frequency
- **communication** patterns

Why capabilities, not roles?

People can play dual roles on teams; understanding capabilities needed first and then discussing team members can help create a suitable team for the work they will undertake while keeping the team small.

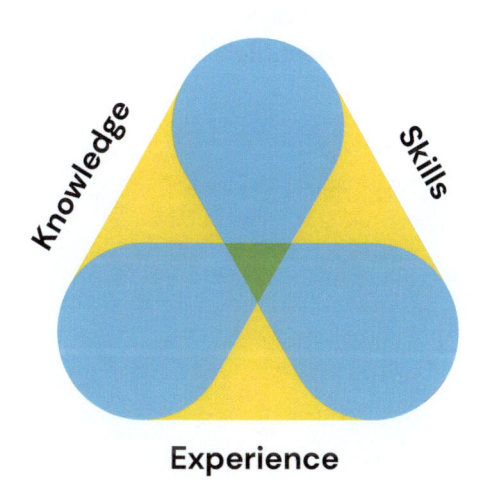

Knowledge Skills Experience

When I say "capability", I mean the application of **knowledge**, **skills** and **experience** to achieve an outcome.

Consider these three aspects:

What **knowledge** does the team need? Are there people who have a deep understanding of the end users or relevant systems?

What **skills** do the team need for the work at the stage it is at? (E.g. technical, analytical, financial, planning, etc)

What level of **experience** does the team need? Is it complex new work that requires a high level of expertise, or something you have done before?

Team size and the onion layers

This theory of team size is closely related to Robin Dunbar's work on human group sizes. You've probably heard of "Dunbar's number". It says that human groups normalise at around 150 people. It's often used to talk about the number of friends in our social circles. It also breaks down further than that, into types of friends in different social layers, which are inner core (**5**), best friends (**15**), good friends (**50**) and friends (**150**).

Dunbar's research also shows that communication patterns between friends correlate to what social layer they are in.[5]

Dunbar says:

"Each layer is three times bigger than the other; so you have an inner, inner core of intimate friends and relations, of about five, and then there's the next layer out, it's about 15. If you like to think of those as best friends, perhaps, they're the people you might do most of your social Saturday evening barbeques with, and that of course includes the five inside. And then this next layer out is 50 (you might think of those as good friends), and the 150, your friends." [6]

I'll reference Dunbar's number in the next section when I talk about creating your Team Onion model.

5   15   50   150

4

Creating your Team Onion

So far, we've looked at the theoretical Team Onion. We know it's a collaborative tool with co-created and co-owned outputs. Its power is in the conversations around it. It helps to uncover assumptions, make decisions and identify actions requiring real-time, synchronous discussions.

Now we're going to make things practical, and directly applicable to you or your team. I'm going to explain how to create your own Team Onion.

It's best to do this in a workshop setting, either face to face on a wall with sticky notes or over video using an online whiteboard like Miro. See teamonion.works/tools for Miro and Mural templates.

It can take a few sessions to go through all the activities, so take your time and don't rush it.

This chapter takes you through the process step-by-step. Feel free to adapt these steps to your own needs.

The five steps to creating your Team Onion

1 Get the right people together

2 Map out your onion rings

3 Prioritise your engagement

4 Engage your wider team

5 Review and iterate

1. Get the right people together

The first step is to agree on who should take part in creating your Team Onion. That will depend on the stage your team is at, and the circumstances you're working in.

Here are some example scenarios:

- If you use the Team Onion to create a new team, then involve people who know the capabilities needed and those who may be involved.
- If you are using it as part of a team kick-off, invite the team's core members and anyone who can help have the right conversations to build out your Team Onion's layers.
- If you are an existing team and using the Team Onion to review how you work, invite the core team and any collaborators you work with regularly to help foster empathy and understanding.

Make sure everyone understands the model before starting the workshop exercise. The tools listed below can help.

2. Map out your Team Onion rings

Each of the Team Onion layers represents a different type of team member; each has different attributes of purpose, time commitment, collaboration, communication and feedback frequency, covered in Table 1 below.

Each ring also has a guide size against it, loosely based on Dunbar's Number; this helps keep teams as small as possible and reduce cognitive load.

Start by drawing your onion's three rings. Then start adding names, starting at the Core and working outwards. Write people's names on sticky notes, and add them to the appropriate ring in the onion.

Encourage the workshop participants to add as many people as they want to. You can discuss, negotiate and reduce the numbers through conversation before agreeing and moving to the next ring.

Capabilities, commitment, collaboration and communication.

When thinking about who to put in the layers, consider the capabilities (knowledge, skills and experience) needed for the team, rather than job titles. For example, instead of saying: "We need to add the Head of Design in this ring, to get design sign-off at every step," say: "We're going to need regular input from a designer with experience in this field, to make sure we're moving in the right direction."

Once you have mapped out all your layers, you can agree on the time commitment and effective collaboration and communication patterns for each member:

Core

At the centre of the onion is the core team; this is the multidisciplinary team with the capability needed to achieve its goal. They need high levels of trust, collaboration and communication; they work exclusively on a specific thing, and they work together every day.

Collaborators

The collaborators are vital to a team's success. They bring in specialist capabilities and ongoing assurance, reduce dependencies, and help to remove blockers. They need to collaborate with the core team, and be in regular communication with them to build trust and empathy. They will need to understand how the team works and what it is trying to achieve. In return, the core team need to understand each collaborators' role and value.

When mapping out your collaborators, you might need to use team names at first, rather than individual names. Aim to replace team names with individual names as soon as possible, though, to help you build good working relationships.

How the core team engages with each collaborator or group of collaborators may differ.

Collaborators will probably be working with more than one team and have other work commitments; this is a benefit as this helps create a network across the organisation.

Supporters

The supporters are the people that help the team succeed by providing support, air cover, alignment or representation. They may be a senior sponsor, a team that work comes from, or an enabling function that doesn't need to collaborate as closely.

This ring is about creating alignment across teams and with organisational goals or priorities. They are not as close to the centre of the onion and will have less regular contact with the core team. However, they are still a crucial extended part of the team and can have a great impact on successful delivery.

This table sums up how to use each ring of the onion:

Core	Collaborators	Supporters
Purpose		
A multi-disciplinary delivery team, working towards a common goal to deliver against a need.	Bring in specialist information, provide assurance, make decisions, and reduce dependencies or blockers.	Provide alignment with organisational goals and other parts of the organisation.
Time commitment		
Full time.	Varying by collaborator, this may change over time as the needs of the delivery change.	Attending alignment meetings, demos and show and tells.
Collaboration, communication and feedback		
Daily.	Regularly to collaborate, build trust and enable the right conversations.	Every fortnight as needed, supported with asynchronous updates.
Size guide		
5-9 people.	4-12 people.	Up to 30 people or teams.

Table 1: The Team Onion rings and attributes

What your team onion should look like

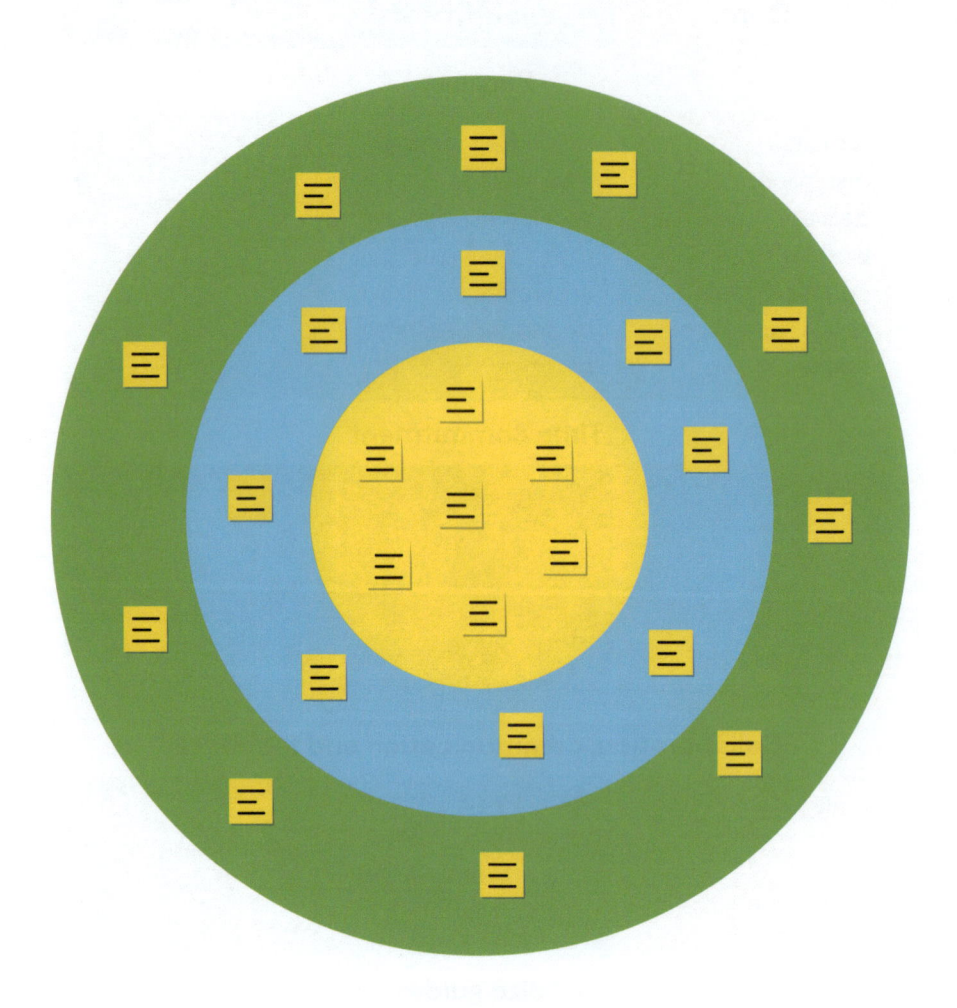

3. Prioritise your engagement

After creating your Team Onion, you may find that you have lots of people you need to talk to; therefore, the next step is to prioritise who to engage with, and work out how manageable all that engagement will be.

Start with any **core** members not already committed and agree on how you will start talking to them if you need to.

Next up, work through the **collaborators**. Identify who the team needs to work with immediately. Then prioritise them with these two questions:

Who will have the most significant impact on delivery at this point in time?

1. Who is the easiest or hardest to engage?
2. Use a chart like the one below to help visualise the prioritisation.

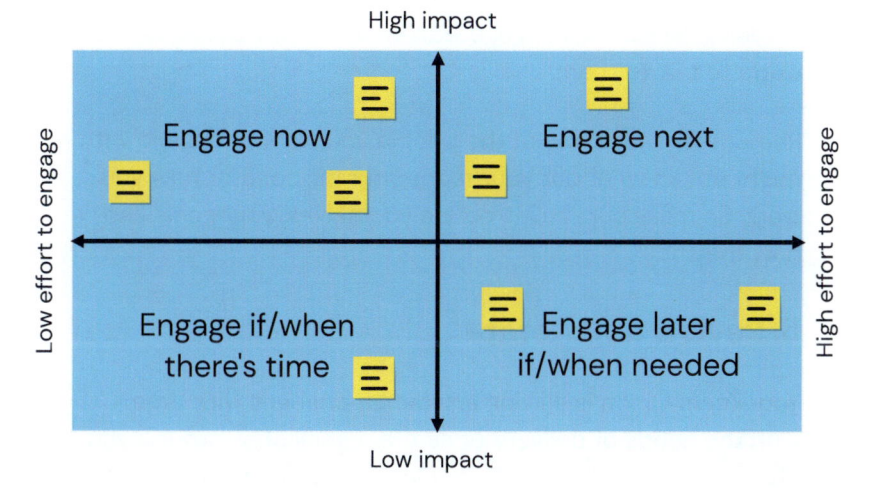

![Prioritisation chart with axes: High impact/Low impact (vertical) and Low effort to engage/High effort to engage (horizontal). Quadrants labelled: Engage now (high impact, low effort), Engage next (high impact, high effort), Engage if/when there's time (low impact, low effort), Engage later if/when needed (low impact, high effort).]

Your priority is to engage with the collaborators in the top left "Engage now" box, those with high impact and low effort to engage. After that, it is the collaborators in the top right "Engage next" box. You can leave the lower impact collaborators to a later date or add them to your regular communications until you are ready to engage with them.

Spend some time within your core team agreeing on the time commitment you'll need from the collaborators at the top of the list, and what role you'd like them to play.

Finally, think about your **supporters**.

Think about communication patterns for your supporters. For example, will you have a regular show and tell, weekly email updates or something else? Are there any supporters that need a different level of communication?

4. Engage your wider team

It's essential to turn your prioritised list into **actions** by agreeing on who will engage with each person. Set some time aside to talk to them.

Remember that some of the people you want to engage with might not know about your team, your purpose, or how you work. So make sure to introduce yourselves, your goals and how they fit in.

5. Review and iterate

Your Team Onion is a living artefact; it changes with time, with the needs of delivery or as the organisation around you changes. So **revisit** your Team Onion regularly to keep it up to date and uncover any emerging assumptions. Before you leave your workshop, put a date in the diary to make sure this happens.

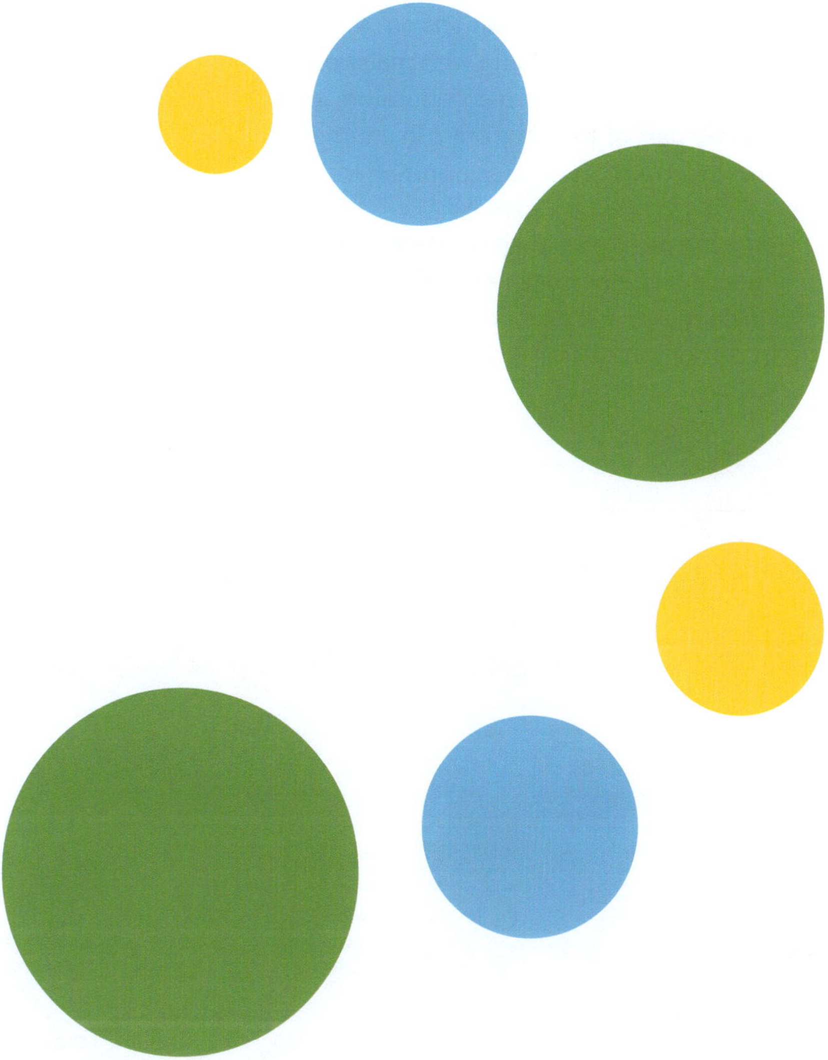

Overlapping Onions

Of course, most organisations are made up of lots of teams, so you'll probably end up with many overlapping Team Onions. People who are collaborators in one Team Onion may also be part of the core team in another. People supporting your team will often be supporting many teams.

Working with more than one team can be a good thing, because it helps information flow across the organisation, which makes things more efficient. Although it also means more complexity for those collaborators.

Be mindful that your collaborators and supporters have other priorities. You may need some coordination to ensure that they aren't overloaded, and everyone is getting the most out of the Team Onion model.

Adapt this model to work for you

Every organisation is different. The Team Onion model is lightweight and intended to be adapted as needed.

Keep to the principles of small teams, breaking down silos, increasing empathy and creating shared responsibility for creating value. Look at the examples in the next section to see how other people have used the Team Onion.

Workshop materials

Check out the Team Onion tools and templates page for supporting material to help you with your workshops teamonion.works/tools

5

Some example scenarios

The Team Onion applies to many different situations depending on what's needed. I launched the model in 2016. Then in 2022, I spent some time talking to people who have been using it so I could share their stories in this book. Here are some of the tips and scenarios I learned.

Building a new team from scratch: getting the right people involved

A common use of the Team Onion is for guiding conversations and decision-making when creating a new team.

One example organisation moved from a more hierarchical team structure to a flatter, more autonomous one. Previously their working practices were fairly siloed. Teams consisted of many individuals contributing to work, but decisions were often made outside of the team by others. Team sizes were unmanageable, which came with significant overhead and slowed things down.

They undertook a new approach to creating multidisciplinary teams focused on a common goal, and the Team Onion helped them do that.

The model helped them frame discussions about what capabilities they needed to achieve their goal. Notably, the guide core team size of 5-9 people enabled sometimes difficult conversations and decisions about who should be on the core team. It also helped to emphasise the need for full-time commitment from them.

They then used the definitions to help the collaborators remain involved and feel like a valued part of the wider team. This expectation setting helped communicate the collaborators' importance and keep them involved while keeping the core team small.

Now when they have a high-level idea of a goal for a new piece of work, they use the Team Onion to build a team around it; and then allow the team to build upon it during their kick-off.

Team kick-off: coalescing a new team

Organisations often start using the Team Onion as part of a team kick-off; it helps teams take ownership of their responsibilities for collaboration and communication.

In one organisation, a new multidisciplinary team came together for a multi-day kick-off. The kick-off activities covered three main areas: understanding the problem space and overarching goals, getting to know each other as a team, and identifying the initial backlog of work.

They started by building out their core team ring of the Team Onion, which helped them learn more about what capabilities each other brings to the team. Then they moved on to listing out everyone who could potentially be a collaborator or supporter and collectively agreed on their expectations.

Through discussion and prioritisation, they focused their collaborator list and decided who in the team would be the contact for each collaborator.

Finally, they used the supporters list to create their show-and-tell invite list.

They used the Team Onion as a living artefact and revisited it when they moved into a new phase or needed to review how things were working.

The Team Onion helped them learn more about each other and proactively engage with the right people.

Team Retrospective: breaking down silos and reducing communication overhead

In one organisation I spoke to, there was a team that many other teams relied on for both new features and technical support. The team was getting so many daily requests for updates from all directions that they had barely any time left to write code. They estimated that they were getting through 15% of their planned work and only spending an hour a week on new features.

They were often delivering less than they had planned, and the less they could deliver, the more urgent the demands became, which in turn gave them less time to do work.

It was leading to animosity, blame and siloed language. They needed a way to manage all the communication overhead, so they reached for the Team Onion.

In their team retrospective, they created a list of everyone they had engaged with recently. They then placed them in the Core, Collaborator and Supporter rings. They used the communication and collaboration frequency to guide them on where to place people.

While creating their Team Onion, they moved everyone they didn't need to actively collaborate with to the supporter ring. They then agreed on what communication patterns allowed them time to focus on work.

They identified a team they collaborate with so frequently that they decided to sit next to them for more natural collaboration.

They also discovered that everyone in the team was working daily with the same person on another team and that this person wasn't working with anyone else, so they moved them into the core.

The Team Onion allowed them to set up better expectations with their supporters and gain back more time to do their work, which meant everyone was happier and they were able to increase time spent developing new features.

Starting a new engagement: building a picture of who's who

One organisation I spoke to uses the Team Onion when beginning a new piece of work with a client.

Many places don't have an up-to-date org chart. When they do, it often shows roles and reporting lines, and doesn't accurately reflect the people and relationships involved, making it hard to navigate. When starting a new piece of work, it helps to map out the people involved as quickly as possible, giving more time to focus efforts on adding value.

This particular organisation uses the Team Onion as an introductory exercise with new clients, to help everyone understand what capability each individual brings to the core team. They then identify people they need to collaborate with or engage as supporters.

They find that writing names down exposes gaps, uncovers teams they weren't aware of, and explicitly calls out who should be on the communication list early on. It also helps to bring out any underlying conflicts, silos or areas where they need to make extra effort to engage people.

It fast-tracks the discovery work of who's who in an organisation and those people who help make the core team successful.

Useful links

Hear from some of the people using and sharing their thoughts on the Team Onion around the web.

The original blog post, Emily Webber (blog post)
emilywebber.co.uk/agile-team-onion-many-pizzas-really-take-feed-team/

Only Dead Fish Neil Perkin (blog post)
onlydeadfish.co.uk/only_dead_fish/2016/05/the-agile-team-onion.html

Learning as part of the Business Analysis community, DWP / Alison Baines (blog post)
dwpdigital.blog.gov.uk/2018/02/27/learning-as-part-of-the-business-analysis-community

Product Managers Handbook, Scott Colfer (website)
scottcolfer.com/product-management-handbook/people.html

The agile comms handbook, Giles Turnbull (book)
agilecommshandbook.com

Service Standard for Wales, Centre for Digital Public Services (website)
cdps-wales.github.io/knowledge-hub/en/service-standard.html

Multidisciplinary teams webinar, Centre for Digital Public Services (webinar)
digitalpublicservices.gov.wales/knowledge-sharing-webinar-multidisciplinary-teams/

Invest in people if you want to transform, Digital Leaders / Colin Banno-Thornton (blog post)
digileaders.com/invest-people-transform

Good Teams need layers like onions, Emily Webber (blog post and book)
https://public.digital/signals/summer-2019/good-teams-need-layers-like-onions

Complementary tools and approaches

Below is a growing list of complementary tools and approaches that can support your teams alongside the Team Onion.

- **Team Manual** emilywebber.co.uk/the-team-manual-a-exercise-to-help-build-empathy-in-teams
- **Impact mapping** impactmapping.org
- **Team Topologies** teamtopologies.com
- **Capability Profile Mapping** emilywebber.co.uk/introducing-capability-profile-mapping

6

References and thanks

References

1. Multidisciplinary in-hospital teams improve patient outcomes: A review ncbi.nlm.nih.gov/pmc/articles/PMC4173201/
2. 'The Agile Manifesto': agilemanifesto.org The Agile Manifesto
3. Diane Coutu (2009).Th 'Why Teams Don't Work': Harvard Business Review; hbr.org/ 2009/05/why-teams-dont-work
4. Agile Team Size – What's the Magical Number? perceptionbox.io/business/agile-team-size-whats-the-magical-number/
5. The costs of family and friends: an 18-month longitudinal study of relationship maintenance and decay Sam G.B. Roberts, Robin I.M. Dunbar 2010
6. You Can Only Maintain So Many Close Friendships theatlantic.com/family/archive/2021/05/robin-dunbar-explains-circles-friendship-dunbars-number/618931

Thanks

The Team Onion is a practical model. I have learnt so much more about it from hearing how other people use it; this has helped inform the content in this book and my own practice. Thank you to everyone that has shared their stories with me.

Special thanks to the people who shared their stories using the Team Onion with me, in no particular order: Jamie Arnold, Chris Fleming, Bronagh McManus, Gary Fleming, Ann Kempster, Stacey Walden, Abisọla Fátókun, Kath Cooper, Hilary Hall, Darren McCormac, Peter Jacobs, Dan Laasna Reuter, Paul Isaacs, Ian Ames and Lianne Mellor.

About the Author

Emily Webber helps organisations create the environment for people and teams to succeed.

She studied fine art at Central St Martins and the Slade School of Fine Art. She uses the approaches she learnt during that time to blend theory and practice into effective methods and models for people-first organisations.

She has worked with creative, digital and technical teams for 20-plus years as a practitioner, mentor, leader and consultant. Her work focuses on joining people up across silos, organisational and professional boundaries, growing professional capabilities and collaborative team practices that enable the delivery of valuable products and services.

As Head of Agile Delivery at the Government Digital Service, she created the widely-followed approach and maturity model for communities of practice and subsequently authored Building Successful Communities of Practice (see tacit.pub/tacitbooks).

She is a popular keynote speaker and event organiser. She has spoken at Mind the Product London, GOTO Copenhagen and Craft. Emily set up Agile in the Ether, Agile Liverpool, Agile in Leeds and Agile on the Bench.

She blogs at emilywebber.co.uk

Works at hellotacit.com

Projects at ewebber.co.uk